Adventure Story Bible
Book 30

Good News
for All Time

Written by Anne de Graaf

Illustrated by José Pérez Montero

Bible Society

Good News for All Time

Contents — Philemon; 1 and 2 Peter; 1 and 2 Timothy;
Titus; Hebrews; Jude; 1, 2 and 3 John; Revelation;
Isaiah 24–27, 34, 54–55

Book 30 — Bible background

In these final parts of the New Testament we are reminded again of how much Jesus cares for every person — whatever they have done, and whatever their position in life. The letters in this book serve as a useful guide to living as a Christian.

Paul's letter to Philemon was written from prison, and is about Philemon's runaway slave who had become a Christian. Paul encouraged Philemon to forgive him and also to accept him as a brother in Christ.

The letters to Timothy and Titus claim to be by Paul, though some people think that someone else has given them their present form.

Timothy was a young man who helped Paul on some of his journeys to spread the Good News. The letters to Timothy give guidelines on how a church should be run, and how to talk about the Good News of Jesus with courage and hope, even in the face of opposition.

Titus also helped Paul on some of his journeys, and the letter to him gives more guidelines on how a church should be run, and how to live as a Christian.

The two letters of Peter encouraged readers — who were scattered throughout the northern part of Asia Minor — to stay close to Jesus even though they were facing persecution and suffering for their faith. They also encouraged the believers to hold to the true teaching of Jesus, and not be led astray by false teachers.

The letter to the Hebrews was written to a group of Christians who were thinking of giving up their faith and going back to the Jewish faith. This was because the opposition to Christianity was becoming so strong.

The letter looks at the Jewish faith, and presents Jesus as the true and final revelation of God, fulfilling many of the Jewish beliefs. The writer encouraged them to stay faithful to Jesus.

The letter from Jude is similar to the second letter of Peter. It encourages the readers not to follow false teaching, but remain true to Jesus.

The letters of John encourage their readers to stay close to Jesus, and not let any wrong teaching take them away from him. John asks them to be faithful, and to love one another.

The Revelation to John was written at a time when Christians were being persecuted because of their faith in Jesus. It was a time of terror as Christians were put in prison and tortured by the Romans.

The writer wants to give his readers hope and encouragement, and urges them to remain faithful. The book contains many revelations and visions which are written in symbolic language that would have been understood only by Christians or Jews. The writer wants the Christians to know that through Christ, God will defeat his enemies, including Satan. Then there will be a new heaven and earth for all his faithful people.

Although it is not clear who wrote some of these letters, the *Adventure Story Bible* has referred to the writers by the names used in the title of each letter.

Here are stories by Christians about the past, present, and future — Good News for all time.

BROTHERS IN CHRIST

The runaway slave

Philemon

Following Paul's dramatic meeting with Jesus on the Damascus road, he had spent many years travelling around telling people the Good News of Jesus' death, resurrection, and love for all. This meant that he was often put in prison because some of the Jews didn't like their faith to be challenged.

While Paul was in prison in Rome, he wrote letters to encourage the many people who had believed in Jesus and become Christians. Not all Paul's letters were written to groups of people, however.

One letter was written to a man called Philemon, who lived in Colossae, in modern Turkey. Paul wrote to him about his runaway slave, Onesimus, who had escaped to Rome.

Onesimus met Paul while he was there, and heard his teaching. What he heard about Jesus changed Onesimus' life so much that he felt sorry for running away. Onesimus chose to believe, and then knew that he should go back to his master.

Paul asked Philemon to welcome Onesimus back, and forgive him for running away. According to Roman law in those days, slaves who ran away could be killed. Paul reminded Philemon that Onesimus was now much more than a slave — he was a brother in Christ.

HOW TO LIVE

When others hurt you

1 Peter 1.1–5.14

The first letter of Peter was to Christians in the area we now call Turkey. It was written at a time when the Roman Emperor had started to persecute and destroy the Christians, and bad times were ahead.

Because the Christians refused to worship the emperor, they were put in prison and killed. They knew that Jesus was their King, the only one they should worship. Many believers were meeting secretly, and the letter from Peter tried to strengthen them for the days ahead. He reminded them that Jesus knew what it was like to suffer at the hands of powerful people.

Even so, Peter wrote, "Respect everyone. Love all the believers, obey and love God, and honour the people who are in charge of you." Peter said it was better to be thrown into prison for doing something right, than for doing something wrong.

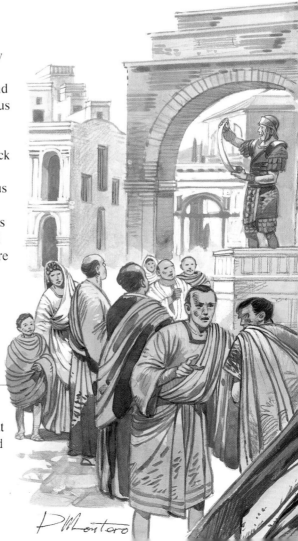

He also asked them to live as God would like them to — loving one another, and being ready for action. He said that it was important to think about who we are inside, and not worry so much about outward appearances.

Real beauty has nothing to do with clothes, make-up, or jewellery. "The beauty that is precious to God," Peter said, "is the sort that shines from inside, from being kind and gentle."

Peter told them to be ready to give an answer to anyone who asked them why they kept hoping when everything looked so bleak. "But when you tell them what you believe, don't talk as if you know more than they do," he said. "Speak gently, and with respect." Lastly, Peter left them with a promise which would also comfort Christians who were suffering in time to come. "When you are suffering," he said, "remember that God will strengthen you, and make you whole."

How to run a church

1 Timothy 1.1—5.25

Timothy had been Paul's special helper for many years. Paul had asked him to join his team of missionaries, and through the years Timothy travelled with him from one town to another. Sometimes Paul sent Timothy out without him, to help and encourage groups of believers.

He was Paul's right-hand man right up to the time when Paul was put into prison in Rome, and he wanted to help other people learn more about Jesus.

This letter sends Timothy greetings and wise advice about how to deal with some of the problems the believers were struggling with.

Paul let Timothy know that with God's help, he could tackle any problem. He tried to encourage Timothy, and warned him to watch out for any wrong teaching which had been going on in the Ephesian church. Paul wanted

Timothy to help the people to know the difference between good teaching and bad.

"Tell them not to pay attention to stories which are not true, or to long lists of ancestors which only produce arguments," he said. "No one is better than another just because of their family. It is faith in Jesus which saves a person."

He also gave Timothy advice about how to choose good leaders and teachers who could help him. They should be people who could be trusted in every way. Paul told Timothy that one way of considering whether people would make good leaders was to look at the way they lived. Were their homes peaceful? Did they owe money?

Paul knew there might be some people in the church who would not like Timothy telling them what to do, as he was younger than most of them. "Don't let anyone try and put you down for being so young," he said. "Instead, be an example in everything you say, think, and do, so that they learn from you. Teach from the Scriptures whenever you can. If you work hard, you will make progress."

Paul reminded him to spend time in prayer, and encouraged his readers to keep praying for everyone — especially those who were in charge — so they might all live quiet and peaceful lives.

If the believers listened to Timothy, they would learn a lot about how to cope with the problems of day-to-day living as a Christian. Paul told Timothy to teach the people to think for themselves and check everything they heard by referring to the Scriptures.

Keep to the truth

1 Timothy 6.1–21

It isn't always easy keeping to the truth. It means more than not telling lies — it means making sure that everything we do and say is done because we love someone, rather than for selfish reasons. It means being honest with ourselves and others. Paul reminded Timothy that this was especially important when teaching other people about God.

He went on to talk about what is most important in life, and about money. "Remember that you're already rich if you are happy," Paul said. "After all, we came into this world with nothing and we'll leave with nothing. All we really need is enough money with which to buy food and clothing."

Paul taught that people who love money too much can cause all sorts of trouble and problems. Some believers who had been greedy for more money were not living in the way Jesus wanted them to. "Instead of chasing after power and money as some people do," Paul said, "chase after what is right. Try to increase your faith, love, commitment, and gentleness." This is what it means to keep to the truth.

"Tell them to be rich in doing good for others," Paul continued. "This is the way to store up real treasure."

Discipline and respect

Titus 1.1–3.15

Titus was another person who helped Paul on his travels. He was a Greek, and a good teacher. Paul had asked Titus to take care of the church on the Greek island of Crete.

This was not an easy mission for Titus. The people of Crete had problems similar to the ones Timothy had in the church in Ephesus. They were struggling with false teaching and pointless arguments. Titus was sent to help them, and choose some leaders for the church.

Paul warned Titus against the false teaching, and against people who made money from preaching. "These people are talking nonsense and must be stopped," he said. "They are upsetting whole families by wrong teaching, just so they can get rich. They say they know God, but you can tell they don't by the way they act."

Paul said that discipline and respect are the signs which show whether or not a person is a true follower of Jesus. Words alone are not enough. They must be backed up by the actions which help faith to grow.

Christians should aim to be calm, and to have real faith. "They should love one another," Paul said, "and be patient and in control of their feelings. They should not be gossips, but hard workers who act sensibly."

Paul warned Titus not to let the Cretans get caught up with the idea that one person was better than another, just because he came from a particular family. That was what had happened to the Christians in Ephesus. "Don't take part in foolish arguments," he said. "They bring you nothing but trouble."

Paul reminded Titus that it is Jesus who saves us, not our own good actions or thoughts. God's mercy was shown in Jesus, and is a gift of his love.

KEEPING THE FAITH
Remaining loyal
2 Timothy 1.1–4.22

In Paul's second letter to Timothy he asked him to remain loyal to the true teaching of Jesus. Paul's first letter had asked Timothy to stay close to the truth, and this was something Paul wanted to emphasize.

He thanked God for Timothy, and said that he prayed for him night and day. "I remember the sincere faith you have," Paul said. "Your grandmother Lois and your mother Eunice had the same kind of faith."

Paul asked Timothy to continue to tell people about Jesus, and to train others to do the same.

Paul went on to remind Timothy that he was working for Jesus, and should stay close to him. In that way he would be able to stand strong and continue preaching.

He warned Timothy that it would be very hard to be a Christian during the last days. "Most people will love only themselves and their money," he said. "They will boast, and be proud and ungrateful. They will gossip and lie, chasing after whatever they want, rather than what God wants. People will listen to them, and never learn what it means to follow Jesus.

"Those who do follow Jesus will suffer at the hands of those who hate him," Paul continued. "But stand steady, and don't be afraid. Bring others to Christ, and continue telling other people what you believe.

"I'm writing this because I won't be there to help you for much longer," Paul said. "Very soon now the time will come for me to stop struggling and go to be with my Lord.

"I have done my best to run the good race of faith," Paul continued. "I have run all the way, and have not stopped trusting in God. At the end of it all there is a great prize waiting for me and all those who run the great race."

It is not always easy to be a Christian, and Jesus never said it would be. Paul said that in the race of faith Christians should train like olympic athletes to be good followers of Jesus. It may be difficult to be like him, but they should never stop trying. They should know God's word and put it into practice, asking Jesus to help them whenever they need strength.

Staying close to Jesus

Hebrews 1.1—5.10

The letter to the Hebrews was written to a group of Christians who were thinking about giving up the Christian faith. Most of them had been Jews, and as opposition to Christianity grew, they thought they might return to Judaism. The writer wants them to stay close to Jesus and his teachings, so he shows the many ways in which he understands Jesus to be the true and final revelation of God.

He starts by reminding them that Jesus is the eternal Son of God, who went through suffering and learnt to be what God wanted. As the Son of God he is superior to the prophets of the Old Testament, to the angels, and to Moses himself — one of the greatest prophets of the Jewish faith.

God was with all of them and they followed him, but Jesus was even closer to God. That is why he died — so that people's sin would be forgiven and they wouldn't be afraid of death any more, because they would have true life.

They must not turn away from this way of life, as some people had turned away from God in Old Testament times. This was something to listen to, believe in, and hold on to.

What is faith?

Hebrews 5.11—13.25

When someone believes in God it means that life changes and becomes new, like being born again. Hebrews reminds the readers that they need to grow and understand what life with God really means. God has promised to help in this, and Jesus is an example of how to live and what is important.

Hebrews continues to encourage the readers to keep following Jesus and grow in faith, by showing that Jesus is the great High Priest. In the past there had been many priests who brought people close to God, but Jesus was the great High Priest who brings people close to him in a new way.

What does it mean to have faith? The writer of Hebrews says that faith is being sure of things we hope for, and certain of things that we can't see. As an example of what it means to have this faith, the writer of Hebrews thought back over the people in history who have trusted God.

He started with Abraham, who trusted God and tried his hardest to do what was right. God promised Abraham and Sarah a child when they were very old, well past the age for having children. Abraham believed, no matter how impossible it seemed. He knew that nothing is impossible for God, and so Isaac was born.

Then he listed many other people who had trusted God, both men and women — Noah, Isaac, Jacob, Joseph, Moses, Joshua, Hannah, Samuel, and many others. They listened to God and did what he asked, however hard it seemed.

The writer of Hebrews thinks of all these people as they are now with God, worshipping him. He wants all people to have this faith to believe in Jesus and his promises, and follow his teaching.

"Jesus is the same yesterday, today, and for ever," he said. God never changes, and as he has loved and spoken to people throughout time, so he will love and speak to people today.

FAITH IN ACTION
Wait in faith

2 Peter 1.1—3.18; Jude

Times had gone from bad to worse for Christians, and pagan emperors and governors captured and killed many Christians. It was very dangerous to let anyone know you were a Christian. Yet that is what believers want to do — share the Good News with others.

The different churches had become confused by false teaching, so the letter reminds the disciples of Jesus to stay true to God and the things that Jesus taught.

"There have been false prophets and false teachers among you," Peter said. "So be careful! Weigh everything you hear against what you know to be true.

"Remember what is written in the Scriptures, and what Jesus and his apostles taught. If you do this, you will know which teaching is from God and which is not."

At that time there were some Christians who thought the world would end soon, and that Jesus would come back to earth again during their lifetime. Because this had not yet happened, some people were saying that Jesus would never return again.

But the way we measure time is not the same as the way God measures time. There is no difference in God's eyes between one day and a thousand years.

The Day of the Lord, the writer says, will happen very suddenly. With a huge explosion the earth would be replaced by a new and perfect world. There will be no sickness or pollution, and God's love and beauty will fill people with joy. God's people will always be close to him, and the whole world will be one family where no one hurts others.

Peter said that until that time they should live as Jesus said they should, and be at peace with God.

The letter from Jude is similar to Peter's second letter, encouraging people to stay true to Jesus' teaching. Jude wrote about what the apostles said the world would be like just before Jesus came back to earth. "Many people will make fun of Christians and what they believe," he said. "They will do this so they can feel free to do whatever they want."

Both these letters warned about people who would want to twist the teachings of Jesus into a shape that suited them. They asked the believers to be careful about how they lived and to love people, and in that way help save them. They also reminded the believers to keep praying.

Live in the light

1 John 1.1—5.21

John's first letter also asks the readers to stay close to the teaching of Jesus and to love one another. John reminded them that Jesus said, "Love one another as I have loved you."

He told them that they needed to stop arguing and doubting. "If we live in the light of Jesus then we will love one another and have peace," he said. "But if we do anything wrong, we will always be forgiven in Jesus' name if we say we are sorry."

Living in the light means living by the truth Jesus taught, loving each other and being kind and honest. It means helping people who need help. Darkness is just the opposite — being selfish, not caring for other people, and telling lies.

John also wrote about how people could tell whether they were living in the light or not. "Whoever says he is in the light, but hates his brother, is really in darkness," he said.

"You can tell who the children of God are because they love others. Don't worry if people who don't believe in Jesus hate you, and don't listen to their lies." John wrote that these people push God further and further out of their lives so they can do whatever they like. They love money and power more than they care about other people.

"Don't just love with kind words," John continued. "Love truly in all that you say and do.

"Remember that the reason we're able to love is because Jesus has first loved us. When you're loving someone in the way Jesus wants you to, you are not afraid. Perfect love throws out fear."

Walk in the truth

2 and 3 John

John's second and third letters were also about the importance of loving. He thought it was the most important rule for living any follower of Jesus could learn.

This is what Jesus had said when someone asked him which was the most important of all the rules God had given us to live by. "Love the Lord your God with all your heart, with all your soul, all your mind, and with all your strength, and love others as yourselves," he said. This was what John reminded the Christians of in his letters.

John said that in doing this we would be living in the truth. Whenever John heard that the believers were living in the truth his heart was full of joy, as it meant that people were loving as Jesus wanted. John was especially happy to hear that the church had been taking care of strangers.

Living in the truth, loving each other, and making people happy, were ways in which the teachings of Jesus would go from one person to another. Sometimes the way a person acts towards a stranger can say more about God than any amount of talking.

JOHN'S VISION OF CHRIST

Special messages

Revelation 1.1—3.22

The Revelation to John was written at a time when Christians were being persecuted because of their faith in Jesus. John wanted the Christians to stay true to Jesus even though they were suffering, and gave them hope for the future.

Revelation is a very difficult book to understand, because it uses symbolic language which only Christians or Jews would have understood.

John wrote that one day he heard a loud voice like the sound of a trumpet. "Write down all that you see and send it to seven churches!" the voice said. Then John had a vision, and saw many strange and beautiful things.

At the beginning of the vision John turned round to see who was speaking, and he saw Jesus standing among seven golden lampstands. His eyes were like blazing fire, his voice was like the sound of rushing waters, and his face was like the sun shining on the brightest of days. In his hand he held seven stars which were seven churches.

When John saw Jesus, he fell at his feet. Then Jesus put his hand on John and said, "Don't be afraid."

Jesus told John to write to the seven churches in Turkey. They are messages to help believers from all times.

Jesus told John to warn these churches that they should take a good, hard look at themselves. Some had forgotten what was most important. "You do not love me now as you did in the beginning," he said to the church in Ephesus. Yet the poorer churches were rich in love, and those who suffered for Christ would be rewarded in heaven.

Jesus also sent a warning to some churches who had become blind to their own problems. Outsiders wanted to hurt them, but the greatest threat came from inside the church. "Those who think you can take care of yourselves are being fools," he said. "If you think you can do everything yourselves rather than rely on God, you're wrong."

Again and again, Jesus told John to call the Christians back to loving, giving, turning to God, and being faithful.

Jesus told John, "I'm here for anyone who asks me into their lives. I'm standing at the door, knocking, waiting for them to hear my voice and open the door. Even when they've done something wrong if they turn to me and say they are sorry, I can help them start again. If they do this I will be with them for ever, and never leave them."

A glimpse of heaven

Revelation 4.1—8.1

During John's vision he saw an open door in heaven, and God sitting on a throne. There was a rainbow around the throne, and it sparkled like a jewel. There were flashes of lightning, and the sound of thunder.

In front of the throne was what looked like a sea of glass, and around the throne were four creatures covered with eyes. The creatures were praising God and singing, "Holy, holy, holy, is the Lord God almighty, who was, who is, and who is to come."

Then John saw that God was holding a scroll. Jesus came and took the scroll and as he opened it, many strange things happened. John was shown that there would be hard times for Christians, but Jesus would guide them, and help them through it.

Then John heard music and saw a huge crowd — the followers of Christ through the ages. No one could count all the people! They were from every race, tribe, nation, and language. They were dressed in white and stood before the throne, waving palm branches. They praised God and sang with the angels, "Praise, glory, wisdom, thanksgiving, honour, power, and might belong to our God for ever and ever! Amen!"

An angel told John in the vision that those who had suffered on earth because they followed Jesus would not suffer once they came to heaven. No one would be hungry or thirsty. The good shepherd, Jesus, would wipe every tear from their eyes and there would be no more reason to cry.

In the future

Revelation 8.2–16.21

In his vision, John also saw many terrible
things happening. He saw glimpses of dreadful
wars, and people being hurt. He also saw that
this would be a time when God's anger would
come on the evil in the world.

There would be terrible earthquakes which
would destroy cities and powerful hail storms
which would ruin crops, but even then the evil
people would not stop doing wrong and turn
to God.

This revelation can make Christians think
carefully about how they live their lives. Are
they doing what they can to make the world a
better place? Are they loving people as Jesus
did? Do they know Jesus' love and acceptance
of them deep inside? Do they realize that at
all times God is asking them to turn away
from wrong, and share the Good News with
others?

A NEW HEAVEN AND A NEW EARTH

God's victory and judgement

Isaiah 24.1—27.13; Isaiah 34.1–17; 54.1—55.13

When John wrote Revelation he drew on many of the ideas and writings from Old Testament times right up to his own day.

Throughout history God had shown his people again and again how much he loved them, and that he would protect them. He would help them in their difficult times and times of suffering, and ensure that justice would be done. He would do things that changed the course of history.

Looking at the stories of the Old and New Testaments it can be seen how God tries to bring people back to him whenever they turn away. And if they do turn away from God they are often unhappy. Things go wrong, and people get hurt. When they turn to God, however, they are able to be positive, and to grow. It is not always easy, but they become the full person they were created to be.

The book of Isaiah also speaks of a time when God would show his anger with the evil in the world, and come to save his people from suffering, making them whole. Like Revelation, it can make people think about how they live, and if they are doing enough for world peace, for a healthy world, and for peace with God and others.

Isaiah and Revelation both show that if people don't think about these things, harm comes to the world. The earth dies because it is not cared for, and people are unhappy because they break laws and can no longer trust each other.

But Isaiah shows that in turning to God, trusting him, and being obedient to him, all this can change. There will be a new earth of peace and justice.

Isaiah and Revelation show that throughout life we have choices to make, and what we decide will have an effect, either for good or for bad.

Only God will be able to judge people's actions and decisions. He loves and knows each person — what they have done, and why. Isaiah and Revelation say that people will be answerable to him. Jesus had also said that it is not for us to judge one another, but for God. It is God who made us and wants to draw us to himself. It is up to us to decide what to do, and be open to change.

Isaiah said that God tells his people, "I will take care of you, and I will love you. The mountains and hills may crumble, but my love for you will never end. I will keep for ever my promise of peace."

Through Isaiah God warned his people, "Turn to the Lord and pray to him now that he is near. Let the wicked leave their way of life and change their way of thinking. Let them turn to the Lord, our God who cares for everyone, and wants to forgive and help them."

God's new world

Revelation 17.1—22.21

John's glimpse of the new heaven and new
earth is the last part of the Bible. It shows
what God's kingdom is like, and makes people
think about whether they are living in that
kingdom. It reminds them about what is most
important in life and whether they are living
as Jesus wants them to.

It also points forward to a time when there
will be no more evil or sin. In John's vision all
the people who were dead came to life again,
and all the believers in Jesus, both past and
present, lived together in heaven.

God was with them, and they saw him. All
the sadness of the past was forgotten, and it
was a new beginning for everything.

In John's vision he saw a new Jerusalem.
He saw it as a great city, with the walls
covered in jewels, and gates of pearl. God was
there, and his presence gave light by night and
day. The streets of the city were made from
pure gold and looked like glass. The water of
the river of life ran through the middle of the
city's street. On both sides was the tree of life,
whose leaves gave healing.

Those who had chosen to follow Jesus were
there with God, and nothing evil was there. It
was a place of light and happiness.

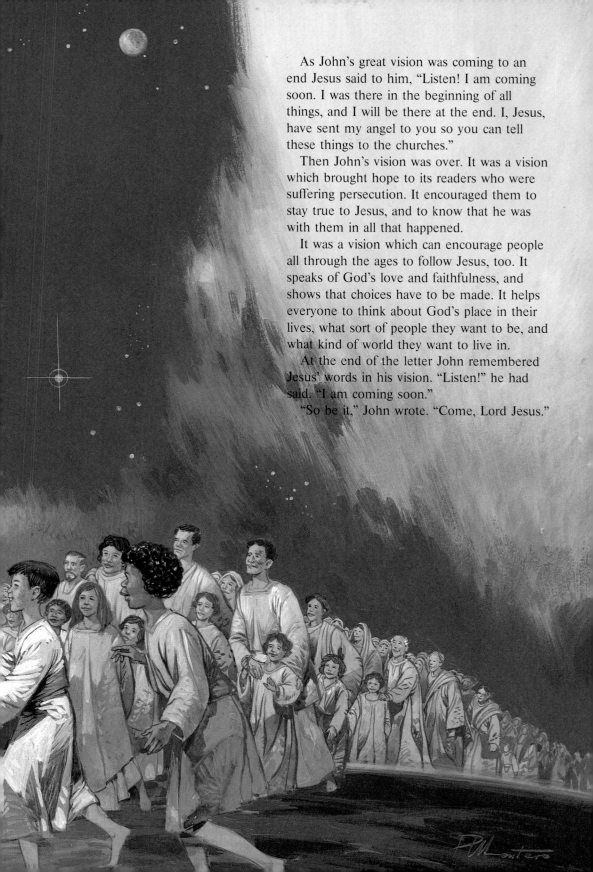

As John's great vision was coming to an end Jesus said to him, "Listen! I am coming soon. I was there in the beginning of all things, and I will be there at the end. I, Jesus, have sent my angel to you so you can tell these things to the churches."

Then John's vision was over. It was a vision which brought hope to its readers who were suffering persecution. It encouraged them to stay true to Jesus, and to know that he was with them in all that happened.

It was a vision which can encourage people all through the ages to follow Jesus, too. It speaks of God's love and faithfulness, and shows that choices have to be made. It helps everyone to think about God's place in their lives, what sort of people they want to be, and what kind of world they want to live in.

At the end of the letter John remembered Jesus' words in his vision. "Listen!" he had said. "I am coming soon."

"So be it," John wrote. "Come, Lord Jesus."

Adventure Story Bible
Old Testament

New Testament